ASSESSMENT GUIDE
Grade 6

Harcourt Brace & Company

Orlando • Atlanta • Austin • Boston • San Francisco • Chicago • Dallas • New York • Toronto • London

Harcourt Brace School Publishers

Harcourt Brace School Publishers

Contents

Overview

In *Your Health*, the assessment program, like the instruction, is student-centered. It allows all learners to show what they know and what they can do, thus providing you with ongoing information about each student's understanding of health. Equally important, the assessment program involves the student in self-assessment, offering you strategies for helping students evaluate their own growth.

The *Your Health* assessment program is based on the Assessment Model in the chart below. The model's framework shows the multidimensional aspect of the program. The model is balanced between teacher-based and student-based assessments.

The teacher-based strand involves assessments in which the teacher typically evaluates a piece of work as evidence of the student's understanding of the health content and of his or her ability to think critically about it. The teacher-based strand consists of two components: Formal Assessment and Performance Assessment.

The student-based strand of the Assessment Model involves assessments that invite the student to become a partner in the assessment process and to reflect on and evaluate his or her own efforts. The student-based strand also consists of two components: Student Self-Assessment and Portfolio Assessment.

There is a fifth component in the *Your Health* assessment program— Daily Assessment. This essential component is listed in the center of the Assessment Model because it is the "glue" that binds together all the other types of assessment.

Your Health ASSESSMENT MODEL

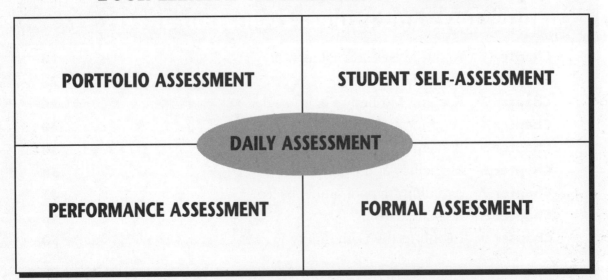

Harcourt Brace School Publishers

Description of Assessment Components

Daily Assessment and Classroom Observation

Daily assessment is central to the assessment program. Ultimately, it is the daily events that are observed and recorded that provide the most comprehensive assessment of student growth. *YOUR HEALTH* provides several ways of helping you assess daily student progress.

- *In the Student and Teacher Editions* every lesson ends with a LESSON CHECKUP. These features provide a mix of factual recall, critical thinking, and skill questions.
- *In this Assessment Guide* a Life Skills Observation Checklist (page 6) can help you evaluate students' skills in health.

Student Self-Assessment

Student Self-Assessment encourages students to reflect on and monitor their own gains in health knowledge, development of life skills, and changes in attitude.

- *In the Student and Teacher Editions* Journal Notes, Set Health Goals, and Use Life Skills are features of every chapter. These features encourage students to reflect on what they have learned and apply their new knowledge to their lives.
- *In this Assessment Guide* you will find a Healthy Habits Checklist (page 8) for students to use in assessing their current level of wellness. The Individual Self-Assessment Checklist (page 9) and the Team Self-Assessment Checklist (page 10) can be used to aid students in reflecting on their performance.

Portfolio Assessment

Students make their own portfolios in Portfolio Assessment. Portfolios may also contain a few required or teacher-selected papers.

- *In the Student and Teacher Editions* every chapter includes a wealth of activities that results in products that can be included as portfolio items.
- *In this Assessment Guide* are support materials (pages 11–15) to assist you and your students in developing portfolios and in using them to evaluate growth in health.

Formal Assessment

Formal assessments can help you reinforce and assess students' understandings of ideas developed in each chapter. Chapter Reviews and Tests require students to reflect on, summarize, and apply chapter concepts.

- *In the Student and Teacher Editions* each chapter ends with a chapter review and test.
- *In this Assessment Guide* is a test for each chapter (beginning on page 18). Answers are shown in reduced form in the Teacher Edition, as well as in the Answer Key on pages 54–62.

Performance Assessment

Health literacy involves more than just what students know. It is also concerned with how they think and how they do things. The Chapter Project is a performance task that can provide you with insights about students' knowledge, skills, and behaviors.

- *In the Student and Teacher Editions* a project is described on each chapter opening page. Periodically throughout each chapter, Project Check-Up tips provide strategies for encouraging students to continue working on their projects. Projects are assessed at the ends of chapters.
- *In this Assessment Guide* a scoring rubric for each project is provided following each Chapter Test. Students can assess their own performance on a project using the Student Project Summary Sheet found on page 17.

Harcourt Brace School Publishers

DAILY ASSESSMENT and CLASSROOM OBSERVATION

In *YOUR HEALTH,* "child watching" is a natural and continual part of teaching and an important part of the evaluation process. The purpose is to record observations that can lead to improved instruction in health. An observation checklist is provided on page 6 for recording student performance on six life skills that are emphasized in *YOUR HEALTH.* These skills are listed and described below. Indicators to help you evaluate each skill appear on the checklist.

❑ **Make Decisions**—the process of selecting among alternatives to decide the wisest thing to do in order to avoid risky situations or health risks.

❑ **Refuse**—selecting and using strategies to effectively react to peer pressure so as to avoid a risky action.

❑ **Resolve Conflicts**—selecting and using strategies to effectively communicate and compromise in order to find solutions to problems or to avoid violence.

❑ **Manage Stress**—acting to relieve the symptoms of stress that occur when physical, intellectual, emotional, or social needs are not met.

❑ **Communicate**—using strategies to transmit information, ideas, needs, feelings or requests in a form that aids interpretation.

❑ **Set Goals**—deciding what improvements to make in one's physical, intellectual, social, or emotional condition and taking action to move toward those goals.

Harcourt Brace School Publishers

Tips for Using
Life Skills Observation Checklist

- Survey the Chapter Organizer, the margin features, and the Chapter Review pages in your Teacher's Edition to identify the life skills developed in a chapter. Then decide which of these features you wish to assess using the checklist.

- Select several students to observe. Often your observations can be more effective if you focus your attention on only a few students rather than trying to observe the whole class at once.

- Don't agonize over the ratings. Students who stand out as particularly strong will clearly merit a rating of 3. Others will clearly earn a rating of 1. This doesn't mean, however, that a 2 is automatically the appropriate rating for the rest of the class. There may be students who have not had sufficient opportunity to display their strengths or weaknesses. In those instances, Not Enough Opportunity to Observe may be the most appropriate rating.

- Use the data you collect. Refer to your observation checklist while making lesson plans, evaluating your students' growth in health, constructing cooperative learning groups, and holding conferences with students and family members.

Rating Scale

3 Outstanding
2 Satisfactory
1 Improvement Needed
☐ Not Enough Opportunity to Observe

Students' Names

✔ **Make Decisions**						
Skill Indicators: The student						
• considers options, risks, and constraints						
• role-plays healthful decision making						
• makes wise decisions in everyday situations						
✔ **Refuse**						
Skill Indicators: The student						
• says *no* in a convincing way						
• suggests healthful alternatives to health-risking activities						
• uses facts to explain reasons for refusal						
• walks away if peer pressure becomes too great						
✔ **Resolve Conflicts**						
Skill Indicators: The student						
• explores options						
• listens attentively to others						
• deals with a problem calmly or makes plans to discuss the problem at a later time						
• walks away if a situation may become violent						
✔ **Manage Stress**						
Skill Indicators: The student						
• analyzes the cause of the stress						
• talks over feelings and seeks help if necessary						
• finds an outlet, such as exercise						
✔ **Communicate**						
Skill Indicators: The student						
• seeks help for problems						
• presents ideas clearly						
• fulfills the purpose of the communication						
• listens attentively to others						
✔ **Set Goals**						
Skill Indicators: The student						
• sets reasonable goals to improve or maintain health						
• makes an action plan to achieve goals						
• is disciplined in following a plan						
• evaluates the results of personal efforts						

Harcourt Brace School Publishers

STUDENT SELF-ASSESSMENT

Researchers have evidence that self-assessment and the reflection it involves can have significant and positive effects on learning. To achieve these effects, students must be challenged to reflect on their work and to monitor, analyze, and control their own learning—beginning in the earliest grades.

Your Health provides three checklists to encourage self-assessment.

- The "Healthy Habits Checklist" allows each student to do a self-assessment of his or her level of wellness. The checklist helps students target health areas to work on throughout the year.
- The "My Thoughts Exactly!" checklist allows individual students to reflect on their work at the end of a chapter.
- The "How Did Your Team Do?" checklist provides an opportunity for a team of students to reflect on how they did after they have worked cooperatively on a health activity or project.

Other opportunities for student self-assessment include Journal Notes and the Set Health Goals and Use Life Skills questions found at the end of each lesson. Note that Journal Notes provide an opportunity for private self-assessment and reflection and should not be used for evaluation or assessment.

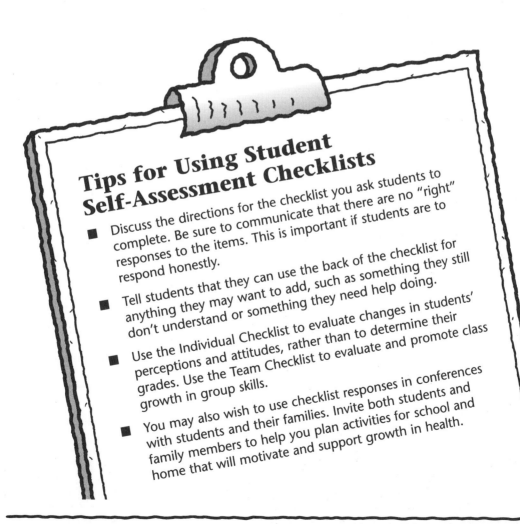

Tips for Using Student Self-Assessment Checklists

- Discuss the directions for the checklist you ask students to complete. Be sure to communicate that there are no "right" responses to the items. This is important if students are to respond honestly.

- Tell students that they can use the back of the checklist for anything they may want to add, such as something they still don't understand or something they need help doing.

- Use the Individual Checklist to evaluate changes in students' perceptions and attitudes, rather than to determine their grades. Use the Team Checklist to evaluate and promote class growth in group skills.

- You may also wish to use checklist responses in conferences with students and their families. Invite both students and family members to help you plan activities for school and home that will motivate and support growth in health.

Name _____ Date _____

Chapter Title _____

Healthy Habits Checklist

This quiz will tell you how healthy your daily habits are. Put a check-mark in the proper column. When finished, add up your score. Take the quiz several times this year and see how your health habits improve!

	ALWAYS	SOMETIMES	NEVER
Using Life Skills			
1. I weigh options and make healthful decisions.			
2. I say *no* if I need to.			
3. I resolve conflicts peacefully.			
4. I use stress-management strategies.			
5. I communicate with others clearly.			
6. I set goals for myself and work toward attaining them.			
Making Healthy Choices			
1. I eat healthful meals and snacks.			
2. I get enough sleep.			
3. I make time for physical activities.			
4. I avoid alcohol, tobacco, and drugs.			
5. I take medicines safely.			
6. I use safety equipment when playing sports and use a safety belt in a car.			
Getting Along with Others			
1. I have some close friends.			
2. I am a responsible family member.			
3. I work well with others.			
4. I apologize when I am wrong.			
5. I feel good about myself.			
6. I get along with other students.			

Give yourself 2 points for each ALWAYS, 1 point for each SOMETIMES, and 0 points for each NEVER. Add up your score for each category.

8-12 points	4-7 points	0-6 points
You Have Healthy Habits!	You Need Improvement	Work to Do Better

Harcourt Brace School Publishers

Name _____ Date _____

Chapter Title _____

My Thoughts Exactly!

Decide whether you agree or disagree with each statement below. Circle the word that tells what you think. If you are not sure, circle the question mark. Use the back of the sheet for comments.

1.	I understand the ideas in this chapter.	**Agree**	**?**	**Disagree**
2.	I found this chapter interesting.	**Agree**	**?**	**Disagree**
3.	I learned a lot.	**Agree**	**?**	**Disagree**
4.	I liked working as a member of a group better than working alone on activities.	**Agree**	**?**	**Disagree**
5.	I contributed my share of work to group activities.	**Agree**	**?**	**Disagree**
6.	I helped others at home and at school.	**Agree**	**?**	**Disagree**
7.	I am getting better at decision making.	**Agree**	**?**	**Disagree**
8.	I make my needs, feelings, and ideas known to my family, friends, and others.	**Agree**	**?**	**Disagree**
9.	I focus more on my strengths than my weaknesses.	**Agree**	**?**	**Disagree**
10.	I practice good health habits.	**Agree**	**?**	**Disagree**

Think about each question below and write a short answer to each one.

11. What did you like best in this chapter? Tell why. _____

_____

_____

12. What would you like to learn more about? _____

_____

_____

Harcourt Brace School Publishers

Name _____ Date _____

Team Members _____

Activity _____

How Did Your Team Do?

Read each item. Mark the number that tells the score you think your team deserves.

How well did your team	High		Low
1. plan for the activity?	3	2	1
2. carry out team plans?	3	2	1
3. listen to and show respect for each member?	3	2	1
4. share the work?	3	2	1
5. make decisions and solve problems?	3	2	1
6. make use of available resources?	3	2	1
7. organize information?	3	2	1
8. communicate what was learned?	3	2	1

Review your answers to 1 through 8. Then answer the questions below.

9. What did your team do best? _____

_____

_____

10. What can you do to help your team do better work?

_____

_____

11. What did your team like most about the activity?

_____

_____

Harcourt Brace School Publishers

PORTFOLIO ASSESSMENT

For portfolio assessment, students make collections of their work. Their portfolios may include a few required papers such as the Project Summary Sheet, Project Evaluation Sheet, and Individual Self-Assessment Checklist. Beyond these, students have the opportunity to add work samples that they believe represent their growth in health.

Portfolios
- **provide comprehensive pictures of student progress.**
- **foster reflection, self-monitoring, and self-assessment.**

The value of portfolios is in making them and in discussing them, not in the collection content itself. Organizers are provided on the following pages to help you and your students make and use them for evaluation.

Getting Started with Portfolio Assessment

■ Introduce portfolios by explaining that artists, fashion designers, writers, and other people use portfolios to present samples of their best work when they are applying for jobs. Explain that the purpose of student portfolios is to show samples of their work in health.

■ Engage your students in a discussion of the kinds of work samples they might choose and the reasons for their choices. For example, the portfolio might include a written work sample, Activity Book pages, and a creative product. Point out that students' best work is not necessarily their longest or their neatest. Discuss reasons for also including a few standard pieces in each portfolio, and decide what those pieces should be. The Project Summary Sheet (page 17), for example, might be a standard piece in all portfolios because it shows the student's ability to use knowledge and skills to solve a problem.

■ Another standard portfolio piece might be the Health Experiences Record (page 13), on which students log their independent health activities, including out-of-school experiences related to health. The Health Experiences Record can reveal student interests and ideas you might otherwise not know about.

■ Establish a basic plan that shows how many work samples will be included in the portfolio, what they will be, and when they should be selected. Ask students to list on A Guide to My Health Portfolio (page 14) each sample they select and explain why they selected it.

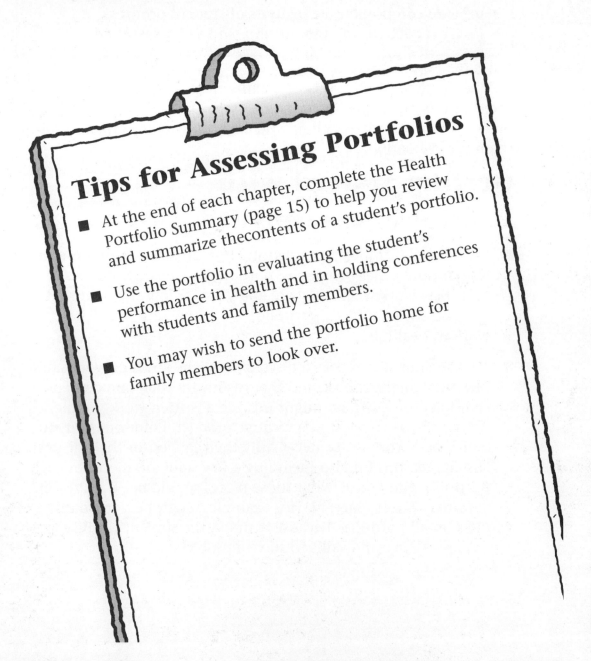

Tips for Assessing Portfolios

■ At the end of each chapter, complete the Health Portfolio Summary (page 15) to help you review and summarize the contents of a student's portfolio.

■ Use the portfolio in evaluating the student's performance in health and in holding conferences with students and family members.

■ You may wish to send the portfolio home for family members to look over.

Name _____

Health Experiences Record

Date	What I Did	What I Thought or Learned

Harcourt Brace School Publishers

Name _____ Date _____

A Guide to My Health Portfolio

What Is In My Portfolio	Why I Chose It
1.	
2.	
3.	
4.	
5.	
6.	
7.	
8.	

I organized my portfolio this way because _____

_____

_____

_____

Harcourt Brace School Publishers

Student's Name

_____ Date _____

Goals	Evidence and Comments
1. Growth in knowledge about health and safety.	_____ _____ _____ _____ _____

2. Growth in using life skills:
  • make decisions
  • refuse
  • resolve conflicts
  • manage stress
  • communicate
  • set goals
	_____
	_____
	_____
	_____
	_____
	_____
	_____
	_____

3. Growth in ability to locate, gather, organize, and communicate information about health.	_____ _____ _____ _____
4. Growth in ability to practice good health habits.	_____ _____ _____ _____ _____

SUMMARY OF PORTFOLIO ASSESSMENT

FOR THIS REVIEW			SINCE LAST REVIEW		
Excellent	Good	Fair	Improving	The Same	Not as Good

CHAPTER TESTS AND PROJECTS

Using Chapter Tests

The Chapter Tests can help you find out how well your students understand, integrate, and apply the important ideas that are developed in each chapter. Included in each test are numerous thought-provoking items that require the student to reflect on and summarize chapter ideas, rather than simply to recall them.

You will find answers to the chapter tests in the Answer Key of this Assessment Guide as well as in reduced form at the end of each chapter in the Teacher Edition.

Follow-up discussion of students' responses to test items is encouraged. Discussion gives students the opportunity to explain their answers. (Creative students may devise an unforeseen solution to a problem or apply concepts in a correct but unexpected manner.) Discussion also helps dispel any lingering misconceptions students may have about the topic.

Using Projects as Performance Assessments

The Chapter Project is a performance task that can provide you with insights about students' understandings, skills, behaviors, and attitudes about health. The project also requires the use of skills such as critical thinking, decision making, and problem solving. You can use the project to evaluate the performance of both individuals and teams.

You may want to read the teacher suggestions for introducing the project a few days before students begin to work on it. Suggestions are in each Introduce the Chapter part of your Teacher Edition.

Before students begin the project, explain how you will evaluate their performance. You may want to use the scoring rubric provided for each project. (See the Project Evaluation Sheet that follows each Chapter Test in this guide.) If so, explain the three-point scoring system in language students can understand.

Distribute and discuss the Project Summary Sheet provided on the following page. You may wish to have students complete this sheet as they work on the project or after they finish it.

Harcourt Brace School Publishers

To Sum It Up

**You can tell about your project by completing the
following sentences.**

1. My project was about _____

   _____

   _____

2. I worked on this project with _____

   _____

   _____

3. I gathered information from these sources: _____

   _____

   _____

4. The most important thing I learned from doing this project is _____

   _____

   _____

5. I am going to use what I have learned by _____

   _____

   _____

6. I'd also like to tell you _____

   _____

   _____

Harcourt Brace School Publishers

Setting Goals

Write the letter or letters of the correct answer on the line at the left. More than one answer may be correct.

_____ 1. Having self-respect is important because it allows you to _____ .
    a. put others down
    b. make decisions that are right for you
    c. take on challenges and try new things
    d. be dishonest about who you are

_____ 2. It is important to know your strengths and weaknesses because _____ .
    a. both strengths and weaknesses make up the real you
    b. your friends will only tell you about your weaknesses
    c. you are not perfect
    d. someone will ask you to list them

_____ 3. Setting goals for oneself is a sign of _____ .
    a. anxiety
    b. adolescence
    c. family support
    d. maturity

_____ 4. Self-control is the ability to _____ .
    a. understand, express, and accept uncomfortable feelings
    b. maintain control over your actions no matter what you're feeling
    c. set goals
    d. trust others

_____ 5. Grief is different from occasional sadness because _____ .
    a. it can't be explained
    b. everyone expresses it differently
    c. you miss the person or pet who has died
    d. it feels very strong and lasts for a while

There are five steps to follow for reaching your goals. Complete the chart below by writing the two steps that are missing from the chart.

You've reached Your Goal!

6.

5 _____

4 | Think about the results

3 | Follow your plan

7.   2 _____

1 | Identify the goal

Harcourt Brace School Publishers

Name _____ Date _____

Write *T* or *F* to tell whether the statement is true or false.

_____ 8. Anger is a feeling that we can always deal with alone.

_____ 9. There are ways to deal with stress once you understand its causes.

_____ 10. Learning how and where to find new friends and how to be a friend takes practice.

_____ 11. Although life is full of changes, we should not expect our friendships to change.

_____ 12. Peer pressure can be positive.

_____ 13. We always have choices about how to deal with conflict.

_____ 14. Sometimes a mediator is necessary to help resolve a conflict.

_____ 15. Only young people have conflicts.

_____ 16. Knowing how to resolve conflicts peacefully sets a good example for others.

_____ 17. When you collaborate, you work alone toward a personal goal.

Cooperation is an important lifelong skill. Write the correct letter on each line to match each term with a real-life situation.

a. stereotype	**b.** prejudice	**c.** diversity	**d.** collaborate

_____ 18. Mike and his family moved to a new neighborhood. He had never known any Asian-Americans until now. Mike thought that all Asian-Americans spoke Chinese and ate with chopsticks.

_____ 19. Maritza and her friends always eat together in the school cafeteria. They never invite other students to sit with them. They never accept invitations from other students to sit at different tables. They refuse to get to know people who are different from them.

_____ 20. Sam lives in an inner-city neighborhood. Many different types of people are his neighbors. They speak many different languages and celebrate many different customs throughout the year. Sam enjoys knowing so many different people.

Name _____ Date _____

Stress in our lives can be managed. List the four steps for managing stress.

21. _____

22. _____

_____

23. _____

24. _____

Identifying the steps in resolving conflicts is important in solving our own conflicts. Find the four steps to conflict resolution among the statements below and write them on the lines.

Listen to all sides of the conflict.	Focus on differences.
List your strengths.	Agree that you disagree.
Know what stress feels like and what causes it.	Avoid the conflict.
Let someone else make all the decisions.	Brainstorm options.
Learn to release tension.	Judge everyone's feelings.
Choose a solution.	

25. _____

26. _____

27. _____

28. _____

Carol is determined to ski this winter after suffering two broken legs in a car accident. She knows that she must go to physical therapy every day, even when she is tired and the therapy sessions are painful. Each evening she rewards herself by having a snack, watching a favorite TV show, or talking an extra long time on the phone with her best friend.

29. Identify Carol's long-term goal.

_____

30. Identify Carol's short-term goal.

_____

Harcourt Brace School Publishers

Name _____ Date _____

Chapter Project Evaluation Sheet (Teacher)

**Rubric for Evaluating Student Performance
on the Chapter 1 Project**

Project: Write a script for an interview
Purpose: To gather and organize information into a script for an interview that shows what steps were followed by a person who has met a personal goal; to develop work skills; to use what is learned from the project in everyday life.

Use the indicators below to help you determine the student's overall score.

Level 3
The student fulfills the purpose of the project in an exemplary way.
_____ Gathers information from a variety of sources
_____ Organizes information into a script that demonstrates a thorough understanding of steps followed by a person who has met a personal goal.
_____ Works alone with initiative or works cooperatively with others
_____ Communicates ideas clearly and effectively through a script for an interview
_____ Demonstrates strong ability to apply the information gained from the project

Level 2
The student fulfills the purpose of the project in a satisfactory way.
_____ Gathers information from more than one source
_____ Organizes information into a script that demonstrates a reasonable understanding of steps followed by a person who has met a personal goal
_____ Works alone with initiative or works cooperatively with others much of the time
_____ Communicates ideas reasonably clearly and effectively through a script for an interview
_____ Demonstrates some ability to apply the information gained from the project

Level 1
The student does not fulfill the purpose of the project.
_____ Gathers insufficient information or uses only one source
_____ Fails to organize information into a script that demonstrates a reasonable understanding of steps followed by a person who has met a personal goal
_____ Lacks initiative when working alone or fails to work cooperatively
_____ Has difficulty communicating clear, complete ideas through a script for an interview
_____ Demonstrates little ability to apply the information from the project

Student's overall score _____

Teacher comments:

Patterns of Growth

Write *T* or *F* on the line at the left to show if the statement about family life is true or false.

_____ 1. Being responsible means that you can depend on others.

_____ 2. Being responsible means that you try to solve conflicts yourself instead of waiting for an adult to solve them for you.

_____ 3. Self-discipline is the ability to control your actions.

_____ 4. Learning to cooperate is an important group skill.

_____ 5. Compromising means that being concerned about your own needs and wants is most important.

_____ 6. One way of resolving family conflicts is by expressing your feelings honestly and respectfully.

_____ 7. During a time of change, all family members react the same way.

_____ 8. The birth of a sibling is always a happy time for every family member.

_____ 9. Divorce is one of the biggest family changes a child can experience.

10. Peter's mom and dad are divorcing. What advice could you give Peter to help him deal with his family's situation?

_____

_____

_____

_____

11. Explain how Susan's abilities to cooperate and compromise can help her and her family adjust to her father's remarriage.

_____

_____

_____

_____

_____

_____

Harcourt Brace School Publishers

Match the statements below with the correct term by writing the term on the line at the left.

ovum	sperm	embryo	fetus	mitosis
nucleus	heredity	inherited trait	genes	
DNA	chromosomes	dominant	recessive	

_____ 12. The process in which the body's cells divide and make new cells

_____ 13. Genes linked together in the cell's nucleus to form long strands of matter

_____ 14. The passing of characteristics from parents to their children

_____ 15. The gene that results in a displayed trait

_____ 16. A cell's control center

_____ 17. Egg cell supplied by the mother in human reproduction

_____ 18. After it is three months old, the baby in a mother's womb

Complete the diagram by filling the blanks with the names for the indicated parts of the endocrine system.

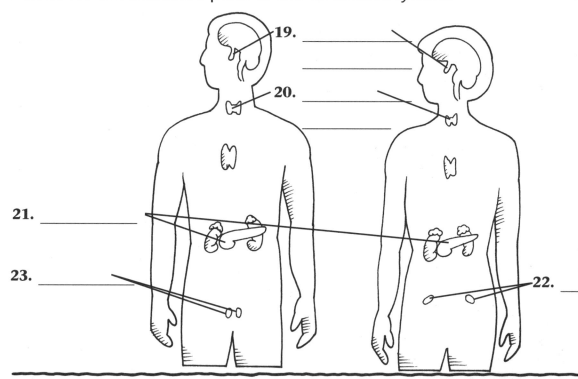

19. _____

_____

20. _____

21. _____

23. _____

22. _____

24. Alberto has just begun puberty. Name two physical changes he may be experiencing.

_____

_____

_____

_____

25. Alberto has noticed that lately he has been very moody. He knows that some of the moodiness has a physical cause. What is the physical change that happens in adolescence that is causing some of Alberto's mood swings?

_____

_____

_____

26. Besides physical changes and mood swings, name one other change Alberto may experience during puberty.

_____

_____

_____

27. Name three healthful choices Alberto can make to keep himself on track during this time of change in his life.

_____

_____

_____

_____

Harcourt Brace School Publishers

Name _____ Date _____

Chapter Project Evaluation Sheet (Teacher)

**Rubric for Evaluating Student Performance
on the Chapter 2 Project**

Project: Make a photo diary of growth and change
Purpose: To gather and organize information to show growth and development over
the years; to develop work skills; to use what is learned from the project in
everyday life

Use the indicators below to help you determine the student's overall score.

Level 3
The student fulfills the purpose of the project in an exemplary way.

_____ Gathers information from a variety of sources

_____ Organizes information to demonstrate thorough understanding of personal growth
and development over the years

_____ Works cooperatively with family members

_____ Communicates ideas clearly and effectively through photographs and labels

_____ Demonstrates strong commitment to applying the information in the diary to
coping with personal growth and change

Level 2
The student fulfills the purpose of the project in a satisfactory way.

_____ Gathers information from more than one source

_____ Organizes information to demonstrate reasonable understanding of personal
growth and development over the years

_____ Works cooperatively with family members much of the time

_____ Communicates through photographs and labels in a reasonably clear and
effective way

_____ Demonstrates some commitment to applying the information in the diary to
coping with personal growth and change

Level 1
The student does not fulfill the purpose of the project.

_____ Gathers insufficient information or uses only one source

_____ Fails to organize information to demonstrate adequate understanding of personal
growth and development over the years

_____ Fails to work cooperatively with family members

_____ Has difficulty communicating ideas through photographs and labels

_____ Demonstrates little commitment to applying the information in the diary to
coping with personal growth and change

Student's overall score _____

Teacher comments:

Health and Fitness

Use the words below to answer the questions about skin and hair. Write the correct word on the line at the left.

epidermis	dermis
oil glands	pores
sweat glands	acne
hair follicles	SPF

_____ **1.** What number indicates about how many times longer you can stay in the sun wearing a sunscreen than you can if you aren't using it?

_____ **2.** What is the name of the protective outer layer of the skin?

_____ **3.** Which glands help keep our bodies cool?

_____ **4.** What do we call the many tiny holes on the surface of the skin?

_____ **5.** What are the tiny sacs from which hairs grow?

_____ **6.** What is the name of the thick layer of skin found below the epidermis?

Match four of the fitness and exercise terms below with their descriptions. Write the letter of the correct answer on the line.

a. muscular endurance

b. flexibility

c. cardiovascular fitness

d. Calories

e. aerobic exercise

f. target heart rate

g. anaerobic exercise

_____ **7.** This term means having a strong heart and circulatory system.

_____ **8.** The ability to bend, twist, and stretch comfortably.

_____ **9.** If you have this type of physical fitness, you can use your muscles for a long time without having to stop.

_____ **10.** This type of exercise is the only exercise that strengthens the heart and lungs and builds cardiovascular fitness.

Name _____ Date _____

11. Explain how the ad below is an example of unhelpful and misleading advertising.

_____

_____

_____

_____

_____

Use these words to label the diagram.

pulp	dentin
enamel	bone
crown	root

12. _____

13. _____

14. _____

15. _____

16. _____

17. _____

Name _____ Date _____

Write *T* or *F* in each blank to show whether the
statement is true or false.

_____ **18.** Another name for tartar is plaque.

_____ **19.** Tartar can build up under the gums and irritate them, leading to
gum disease.

_____ **20.** Dentists recommend you brush your teeth twice a day and floss
once a day.

_____ **21.** When the bacteria in plaque act on sugars in the food you eat, they
produce dentin.

From the list below choose two parts of the eye and
explain how they help us see.

iris	lens	retina

22. _____

_____

23. _____

_____

24. José enjoys playing basketball with his friends at an outdoor basketball court.
He also wears glasses. Name one thing José could do to help protect his eyes.

_____

_____

_____

25. Jennifer mows lawns during the summer to earn extra money. The lawn mower
she uses has a very loud motor. Jennifer sometimes mows as many as five lawns
a day. What could Jennifer do to help protect her hearing?

_____

_____

_____

Harcourt Brace School Publishers

Name _____ Date _____

Chapter Project Evaluation Sheet (Teacher)

**Rubric for Evaluating Student Performance
on the Chapter 3 Project**

Project: Analyze health product ads
Purpose: To gather and organize information to analyze health product ads; to develop
work skills; to use what is learned from the project in everyday life

Use the indicators below to help you determine the student's overall score.

Level 3
The student fulfills the purpose of the project in an exemplary way.

_____ Gathers information from a variety of sources

_____ Organizes information to demonstrate a thorough understanding of the information
in health product ads

_____ Works alone with initiative or works cooperatively with others

_____ Communicates ideas clearly and effectively through a chart of information on the
products and through a paragraph describing the best buy

_____ Demonstrates strong commitment to reading health product ads carefully

Level 2
The student fulfills the purpose of the project in a satisfactory way.

_____ Gathers information from more than one source

_____ Organizes information to demonstrate a reasonable understanding of the
information in health product ads

_____ Works alone with initiative or works cooperatively with others much of the time

_____ Communicates ideas in a reasonably clear and effective way through a chart of
information on the products and through a paragraph describing the best buy

_____ Demonstrates some commitment to reading health product ads carefully

Level 1
The student does not fulfill the purpose of the project.

_____ Gathers insufficient information or uses only one source

_____ Fails to organize information to demonstrate a reasonable understanding of the
information in health product ads

_____ Lacks initiative when working alone or fails to work cooperatively

_____ Has difficulty communicating clear, complete ideas through a chart of information
on the products and through a paragraph describing the best buy

_____ Demonstrates little commitment to reading health product ads carefully

Student's overall score _____

Teacher comments:

Preparing Healthful Foods

The nutrients in our food help keep us healthy. Match the words below to the sentences. Write the correct letters on the lines in front of the sentences.

a. carbohydrates	e. fats	i. vitamins
b. fiber	f. cholesterol	j. water
c. glucose	g. proteins	
d. sucrose	h. minerals	

_____ 1. These nutrients help build and repair cells and give energy.

_____ 2. This substance is found in animal fats and can build up in blood vessels and cause heart disease.

_____ 3. This nutrient is essential for life and is found throughout the body.

_____ 4. These nutrients break down quickly and give energy.

_____ 5. This simple carbohydrate is made from sugar cane or sugar beets and breaks down into glucose in the body.

_____ 6. This substance has no nutrients of its own but helps move food through the digestive system.

_____ 7. These nutrients help cause specific reactions in the body.

_____ 8. This sugar breaks down in the cells to release energy.

_____ 9. These nutrients help the body grow and work. Calcium and iron are two examples.

_____ 10. These nutrients have the most Calories per gram of food and are important for normal body function.

Harcourt Brace School Publishers

Name _____ Date _____

Label each section of the Food Guide Pyramid and explain how each food group helps us stay healthy.

11. _____
   _____
   _____

12. _____   13. _____
   _____   _____
   _____   _____
   _____   _____
   _____   _____
   _____   _____
   _____   _____

14. _____   15. _____
   _____   _____
   _____   _____
   _____   _____

16. _____
   _____
   _____
   _____
   _____

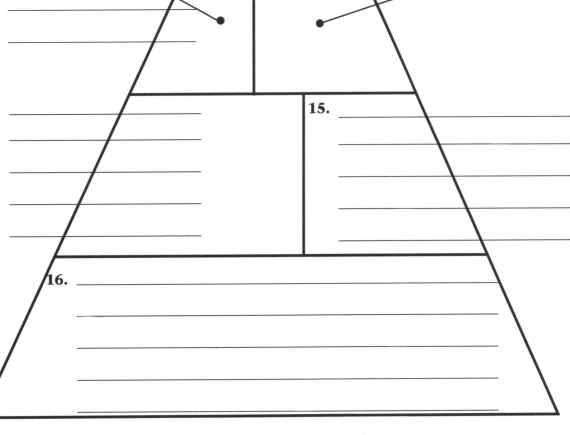

Our bodies have nutritional needs that must be met or serious medical problems can occur. On the lines below, tell what might happen if a person did not receive sufficient amounts of

17. iron _____

_____

18. calcium _____

_____

19. Vitamin A _____

_____

20. Vitamin C _____

_____

Write *T* or *F* to tell if the statements are true or false.

_____ **21.** Many convenience foods spoil quickly because they contain no additives or preservatives.

_____ **22.** Convenience foods are foods that are partly or completely prepared when you buy them.

_____ **23.** By law all packaged foods have protein and carbohydrates.

_____ **24.** Contamination of foods can occur when foods are exposed to harmful substances.

_____ **25.** Washing one's hands with soap and water before preparing a meal can greatly reduce food contamination.

_____ **26.** Pathogens are a serious cause of contamination.

_____ **27.** The sell-by date stamped on foods is a calendar date important only to supermarkets and other types of grocery stores.

_____ **28.** Most spices come from chemicals and artificial substances.

Harcourt Brace School Publishers

Name _____ Date _____

Chapter Project Evaluation Sheet (Teacher)

**Rubric for Evaluating Student Performance
on the Chapter 4 Project**

Project: Design a food poster
Purpose: To gather and organize information about foods; to develop work skills; to use
what is learned from the project in everyday life

Use the indicators below to help you determine the student's overall score.

Level 3
The student fulfills the purpose of the project in an exemplary way.

_____ Gathers information from a variety of sources

_____ Organizes information to demonstrate a thorough understanding of at least
five foods

_____ Works alone with initiative or works cooperatively with others

_____ Communicates ideas clearly and effectively through a poster

_____ Demonstrates strong ability to apply the information from the poster to a personal
commitment to eating nutritious foods

Level 2
The student fulfills the purpose of the project in a satisfactory way.

_____ Gathers information from more than one source

_____ Organizes information to demonstrate a reasonable understanding of two or
three foods

_____ Works alone with initiative or works cooperatively with others much of the time

_____ Communicates ideas reasonably effectively through a poster

_____ Demonstrates some ability to apply the information from the poster to a personal
commitment to eating nutritious foods

Level 1
The student does not fulfill the purpose of the project.

_____ Gathers insufficient information or uses only one source

_____ Fails to organize information to demonstrate a reasonable understanding of one
nutritious food

_____ Lacks initiative when working alone or fails to work cooperatively

_____ Has difficulty communicating clear, complete ideas through a poster

_____ Demonstrates little ability to apply the information from the poster to a personal
commitment to eating nutritious foods

Student's overall score _____

Teacher comments:

Name _____ Date _____

Controlling Disease

Write the letter of the best answer on the line
on the left.

_____ 1. The passing of traits from parents to their children
is called _____ .
a. health risk factor   b. behavior risk factors
c. heredity   d. heredity risk factors

_____ 2. An organism that infects people and makes them ill
is called a _____ .
a. pathogen   b. health risk factor
c. disability   d. trait

_____ 3. Anything that can increase your chances of becoming ill
is known as a _____ .
a. disease   b. health risk factor
c. symptom   d. infection

_____ 4. A condition that damages or weakens part of the body
is called a _____ .
a. infection   b. symptom
c. pathogen   d. disease

_____ 5. Inherited risk factors that increase your chances of becoming ill
are called _____ .
a. environmental health factors   b. behavioral health factors
c. hereditary risk factors   d. individual risk factors

_____ 6. Your body's first line of defense against the pathogens around you
is made up of your _____ .
a. heart and lungs   b. skin and mucous membranes
c. stomach and liver   d. nerves and muscles

_____ 7. Two kinds of STDs are _____ .
a. measles and mumps   b. colds and flu
c. pneumonia and chicken pox   d. gonorrhea and syphilis

_____ 8. Today there are more than 70 different _____ used to treat diseases.
a. antibiotics   b. antibodies
c. antiseptics   d. allergens

Harcourt Brace School Publishers

Name _____ Date _____

Decide in which box the following terms about infectious diseases belong, and write the terms on the lines provided in each box.

9. influenza	**10.** viruses	**11.** protozoa	**12.** common cold
13. fungi	**14.** AIDS	**15.** hepatitis	

CAUSES OF INFECTIOUS DISEASES	TYPES OF INFECTIOUS DISEASES
_____	_____
_____	_____
_____	_____
_____	_____

Write *T* or *F* to show if the statements are true or false.

_____ **16.** Your body's natural ability to fight pathogens is called immunization.

_____ **17.** One kind of white blood cell that makes antibodies is called a lymphocyte.

_____ **18.** The body's memory of how to make antibodies to a specific pathogen is called immunity.

_____ **19.** A medicine used to protect people from a certain disease is called an injection.

_____ **20.** An antibiotic is a medicine that kills pathogens, especially bacteria.

_____ **21.** Alexander Fleming discovered the first antibiotic called bacterium.

_____ **22.** The thymus and the spleen produce lymphocytes that produce antibodies.

_____ **23.** A chronic disease is noninfectious and long-lasting.

_____ **24.** All vaccines must be given only once to maintain immunity to a certain pathogen.

_____ **25.** Wash your hands often when you have a cold.

Harcourt Brace School Publishers

Name _____ Date _____

Match the terms related to chronic diseases below with their descriptions by writing the terms on the lines on the left.

cardiovascular diseases	tumor
carcinogens	insulin

_____ **26.** a substance that helps move the sugar in the blood into the body's cells

_____ **27.** chronic diseases of the heart and blood vessels

_____ **28.** things that cause cancer

_____ **29.** an abnormal mass of cells

Name five lifestyle choices you could make to lower your risk of developing diseases.

30. _____

_____

_____

31. _____

_____

_____

32. _____

_____

_____

33. _____

_____

_____

34. _____

_____

_____

Harcourt Brace School Publishers

Name _____ Date _____

Chapter Project Evaluation Sheet (Teacher)

Rubric for Evaluating Student Performance on the Chapter 5 Project

Project: Make a disease awareness bulletin board
Purpose: To gather and organize information on diseases; to develop work skills; to use what is learned from the project in everyday life

Use the indicators below to help you determine the student's overall score.

Level 3
The student fulfills the purpose of the project in an exemplary way.

_____ Gathers information from a variety of sources

_____ Organizes information to demonstrate a thorough understanding of the causes of a specific disease, the number of cases of the disease in the United States, and the various treatments

_____ Works alone with initiative or works cooperatively with others

_____ Communicates ideas clearly and effectively through a bulletin board display

_____ Demonstrates strong commitment to disease prevention through healthful habits

Level 2
The student fulfills the purpose of the project in a satisfactory way.

_____ Gathers information from more than one source

_____ Organizes information to demonstrate a reasonable understanding of the causes of a specific disease, the number of cases of the disease in the United States, and the various treatments

_____ Works alone with initiative or works cooperatively with others much of the time

_____ Communicates ideas in a reasonably clear and effective way through a bulletin board display

_____ Demonstrates some commitment to disease prevention through healthful habits

Level 1
The student does not fulfill the purpose of the project.

_____ Gathers insufficient information or uses only one source

_____ Fails to organize information to demonstrate a reasonable understanding of the causes of a specific disease, the number of cases of the disease in the United States, and the various treatments

_____ Lacks initiative when working alone or fails to work cooperatively

_____ Has difficulty communicating clear, complete ideas through use of a bulletin board display

_____ Demonstrates little commitment to disease prevention through healthful habits

Student's overall score _____
Teacher comments:

Name _____ Date _____

Drugs and Health

Use the terms below to describe each statement about medicines, drugs, and drug abuse. Write the correct term on the line at the left.

expiration date	medicines	drug
drug dependence	withdrawal	dosage
prescription medicines	side effects	tolerance
over-the-counter medicines	peer pressure	addiction

_____ **1.** Feeling the need for drugs the way other people feel they need food and sleep

_____ **2.** Unwanted reactions that a person might have to a medicine

_____ **3.** Medicines that may be bought without a prescription

_____ **4.** The amount of medicine a person should take

_____ **5.** The feeling that drugs are necessary in order to feel normal

_____ **6.** Any substance other than food that causes changes in the way the body or mind works

_____ **7.** Medicines that may be bought only after a doctor has written an order for them

_____ **8.** Drugs that prevent, treat, or cure health problems

_____ **9.** The need for larger and more frequent doses of a drug to get the same effect

_____ **10.** The body's physical reaction to not getting a drug

Harcourt Brace School Publishers

Name _____ Date _____

Write *T* or *F* to show if the statements are true or false.

_____ **11.** Marijuana and hashish are made from the hemp, or cannabis, plant.

_____ **12.** Marijuana is six to ten times stronger than hashish.

_____ **13.** Marijuana lowers body temperature and makes the heart beat faster.

_____ **14.** Morphine, codeine, and heroin are all powerful drugs made from the sap of the opium poppy plant.

_____ **15.** Hallucinogens are substances that give off fumes people sniff deeply to get high.

Complete the chart below with information on the serious health problems the stimulants and depressants listed can cause.

Stimulants	Depressants	Possible Health Problems
16. caffeine		
17. cocaine		
	18. tranquilizers	
	19. sedatives	

Name five possible effects of drug abuse.

20. _____

_____

21. _____

_____

22. _____

_____

23. _____

_____

24. _____

_____

List one short-term and one long-term effect inhalants
can have on a person's body.

25. Short-term effect: _____

_____

26. Long-term effect: _____

_____

Name two kinds of hallucinogenic drugs.

27. _____

28. _____

Name one reason you should avoid drugs.

29. _____

_____

_____

_____

Harcourt Brace School Publishers

Name _____ Date _____

Chapter Project Evaluation Sheet (Teacher)

Rubric for Evaluating Student Performance
on the Chapter 6 Project

Project: Design an ad campaign
Purpose: To gather and organize information to design an ad campaign; to develop work skills; to use what is learned from the project in everyday life

Use the indicators below to help you determine the student's overall score.

Level 3
The student fulfills the purpose of the project in an exemplary way.

_____ Gathers information from a variety of sources

_____ Organizes information for an advertising campaign that demonstrates thorough understanding of reasons for using medicines wisely or for not using harmful drugs

_____ Works alone with initiative or works cooperatively with others

_____ Communicates ideas clearly and effectively through the design for an advertising campaign

_____ Demonstrates strong commitment to apply the information gained from the project

Level 2
The student fulfills the purpose of the project in a satisfactory way.

_____ Gathers information from more than one source

_____ Organizes information for an advertising campaign that demonstrates reasonable understanding of reasons for using medicines wisely or for not using harmful drugs

_____ Works alone with initiative or works cooperatively with others much of the time

_____ Communicates ideas somewhat clearly and effectively through the design for an advertising campaign

_____ Demonstrates some commitment to apply the information gained from the project

Level 1
The student does not fulfill the purpose of the project.

_____ Gathers insufficient information and/or uses only one source

_____ Fails to organize information for an advertising campaign to demonstrate adequate understanding of reasons for using medicines wisely or for not using harmful drugs

_____ Lacks initiative when working alone or fails to work cooperatively

_____ Has difficulty communicating clear, complete ideas through the design for an advertising campaign

_____ Demonstrates little commitment to apply the information gained from the project

Student's overall score _____

Teacher comments:

Name _____ Date _____

Tobacco and Alcohol

Write *T* or *F* if the statement is true or false.

_____ **1.** Tobacco is a leafy plant from which tar is made.

_____ **2.** Nicotine is a dangerous addictive substance found in tobacco leaves.

_____ **3.** Carbon monoxide is a poisonous gas that takes the place of oxygen in the body.

_____ **4.** The black sticky grime left by smoking is called tar.

_____ **5.** Tars collect on your lungs and air passages, making breathing more difficult.

_____ **6.** Tobacco affects a smoker immediately.

_____ **7.** Only the lungs are affected by smoking.

_____ **8.** A smoker's body absorbs vitamins and nutrients as well as the body of a nonsmoker.

_____ **9.** Nicotine increases the production of stomach acid, which may contribute to ulcers.

_____ **10.** Smokers are four times less likely to develop heart disease.

11. Explain how environmental tobacco smoke can affect nonsmokers.

_____

_____

_____

Smokeless tobacco can also be very dangerous. Name two ways in which smokeless tobacco can injure a person.

12. _____

_____

13. _____

_____

Harcourt Brace School Publishers

Name _____ Date _____

Name two ways smokers can get help to quit smoking
or using smokeless tobacco.

14. _____

_____

15. _____

_____

Write the letter of the best answer on the line to
complete the statements below on the dangers of
alcohol use.

_____ 16. Unlike food, alcohol is absorbed directly into the _____ .
    a. stomach   b. blood stream
    c. intestines   d. brain

_____ 17. The amount of alcohol in a person's body is called _____ .
    a. intoxication   b. blood depressants
    c. cirrhosis   d. blood alcohol level

_____ 18. Alcohol is a
    a. stimulant   b. barbituate
    c. depressant   d. nutrient

_____ 19. People who are dependent on alcohol need to drink it to feel _____ .
    a. ill   b. addicted
    c. normal   d. dependent

_____ 20. More than four out of ten _____ are alcohol-related.
    a. car crashes   b. broken bones
    c. fires   d. heart diseases

_____ 21. People who suffer from alcoholism drink _____ .
    a. to forget their problems   b. when they feel happy
    c. when they feel sad or   d. all of the above
       disappointed

_____ 22. The disease that allows scar tissue to build up on a person's liver is called
    a. cirrhosis   b. ulcers
    c. larynx   d. pancreas

_____ 23. Cirrhosis can cause the liver to stop processing _____ .
    a. speech   b. proteins
    c. blood   d. nicotine

If someone offers you alcohol, what are three ways in which you could refuse it?

24. _____

_____

25. _____

_____

26. _____

_____

Advertisements for tobacco and alcohol don't always tell the whole story. Name two things these ads might leave out regarding the dangers of these substances.

27. _____

_____

_____

_____

28. _____

_____

_____

_____

What kinds of help can each of the following provide for alcohol problems?

29. alcohol abuse counselors _____

_____

_____

30. Al–Anon _____

_____

_____

Harcourt Brace School Publishers

Name _____ Date _____

Chapter Project Evaluation Sheet (Teacher)

**Rubric for Evaluating Student Performance
on the Chapter 7 Project**

Project: Make a flip book
Purpose: To gather and organize information to show the effects of alcohol or tobacco
on the body; to develop work skills; to use what is learned from the project in
everyday life

Use the indicators below to help you determine the student's overall score.

Level 3
The student fulfills the purpose of the project in an exemplary way.

_____ Gathers information from a variety of sources

_____ Organizes information to demonstrate a thorough understanding of the effects of
alcohol or tobacco on the body

_____ Works alone with initiative or works cooperatively with others

_____ Communicates ideas clearly and effectively through a flip book

_____ Demonstrates strong ability to apply the information in the flip book to a personal
commitment to avoid drinking alcohol and using tobacco

Level 2
The student fulfills the purpose of the project in a satisfactory way.

_____ Gathers information from more than one source

_____ Organizes information to demonstrate a reasonable understanding of the effects of
alcohol or tobacco on the body

_____ Works alone with initiative or works cooperatively with others much of the time

_____ Communicates ideas reasonably, clearly, and effectively through a flip book

_____ Demonstrates some ability to apply the information in the flip book to a personal
commitment to avoid drinking alcohol and using tobacco

Level 1
The student does not fulfill the purpose of the project.

_____ Gathers insufficient information or uses only one source

_____ Fails to organize information to demonstrate adequate understanding of the effects
of alcohol or tobacco on the body

_____ Lacks initiative when working alone or fails to work cooperatively

_____ Has difficulty communicating clear, complete ideas through a flip book

_____ Demonstrates little ability to apply the information in the flip book to a personal
commitment to avoid drinking alcohol and using tobacco

Student's overall score _____
Teacher comments:

Name _____ Date _____

Safety and First Aid

Write the letter of the best answer on the lines to
complete the home and water safety statements below.

_____ 1. When a person touches any part of an electrical circuit, this connection
causes a painful jolt called an _____ .
  a. electric socket   b. electric strip
  c. electric shock   d. electric current

_____ 2. Electricity can pass very easily through _____ .
  a. rubber   b. plastic   c. skin   d. water

_____ 3. When something burns easily, it is said to be _____ .
  a. flammable   b. electrical   c. frayed   d. detectable

_____ 4. Some outdoor fire hazards are fireworks, holiday decorations, flammable
liquids, grills, and _____ .
  a. power tools   b. guns
  c. furniture cushions   d. oily rags and trash

_____ 5. Guns should be kept unloaded in a case that is _____ .
  a. locked   b. unlocked   c. handled   d. plastic

_____ 6. Most cleaning products are very harmful if _____ .
  a. used   b. swallowed   c. touched   d. destroyed

_____ 7. Two keys to water safety are knowing how to swim and _____ .
  a. using a life jacket   b. swimming alone
  c. knowing how to fish   d. knowing how to dive

_____ 8. One way you can increase your chances of survival if you are caught in
deep, warm water is called _____ .
  a. treading water   b. wading
  c. bobbing   d. survival floating

_____ 9. A float plan that includes information on where you plan to go and _____
should be left on shore with a responsible adult when you go boating.
  a. what you will do there   b. when you will return
  c. when you plan to arrive   d. when you will arrive
     and return

_____ 10. If you fall into cold water, do *not* _____ .
  a. leave your clothes on   b. pull your knees up to your chest
  c. tread water   d. breathe

Harcourt Brace School Publishers

Organize the following items by placing them in the family emergency supply kit or in the family first-aid kit. Some listed items do not belong in either kit.

plastic bags	bandages
water	hand cleaner and wipes
scissors and tweezers	blankets
canned food	frozen packaged food
extra clothing	lightbulbs
antiseptic ointment	electric heater
battery-powered radio and extra batteries	

Emergency Supply Kit   **First-Aid Kit**

11. _____   16. _____

12. _____   17. _____

13. _____   18. _____

14. _____   19. _____

15. _____   20. _____

_____   _____

Match the following natural disasters with their correct descriptions. Write the letters on the lines in front of the descriptions. Then write one safety measure that should be taken for each type of natural disaster.

a. earthquake	d. blizzard
b. electrical storm	e. tornado
c. flood	f. hurricane

_____ **21.** This is a violent storm with strong winds and heavy rain that forms over a warm ocean.

_____

_____

_____

_____ **22.** This is a strong rolling, shaking, or sliding of the ground.

_____

_____

_____

_____ **23.** This is an extremely strong windstorm.

_____

_____

_____

Knowing basic first aid for common injuries and medical conditions can save lives. Explain the proper first aid that could be given to a person suffering from *two* of the following injuries or conditions.

sprain	hypothermia	burns	choking

24. _____

_____

_____

25. _____

_____

_____

Gangs are everywhere. List three steps a person could take to help avoid conflicts with gangs.

26. _____

_____

27. _____

_____

28. _____

_____

Harcourt Brace School Publishers

Chapter Project Evaluation Sheet (Teacher)

Chapter
8

Rubric for Evaluating Student Performance on the Chapter 8 Project

Project: Make a safety booklet
Purpose: To gather and organize information and pictures to show preventative and first-aid safety tips; to develop work skills; to use what is learned from the project in everyday life

Use the indicators below to help you determine the student's overall score.

Level 3
The student fulfills the purpose of the project in an exemplary way.

_____ Gathers information from a variety of sources

_____ Organizes information to demonstrate a thorough understanding of preventative and first-aid safety tips

_____ Works alone with initiative or works cooperatively with others

_____ Communicates ideas clearly and effectively through a safety booklet

_____ Demonstrates strong ability to apply the information in the safety booklet to everyday life

Level 2
The student fulfills the purpose of the project in a satisfactory way.

_____ Gathers information from more than one source

_____ Organizes information to demonstrate a reasonable understanding of preventative and first-aid safety tips

_____ Works alone with initiative or works cooperatively with others much of the time

_____ Communicates ideas reasonably clearly and effectively through a safety booklet

_____ Demonstrates some ability to apply the information in the safety booklet to everyday life

Level 1
The student does not fulfill the purpose of the project.

_____ Gathers insufficient information or uses only one source

_____ Fails to organize information to demonstrate adequate understanding of preventative and first-aid safety tips

_____ Lacks initiative when working alone or fails to work cooperatively

_____ Has difficulty communicating clear, complete ideas through a safety booklet

_____ Demonstrates little ability to apply the information in the safety booklet to everyday life

Student's overall score _____
Teacher comments:

Community Health

Write *T* or *F* to show whether the statement is true
or false.

_____ **1.** Tornadoes are hurricanes that form over land.

_____ **2.** Damage caused by a hurricane can cover many square miles.

_____ **3.** A natural disaster is caused by people who waste or misuse
natural resources.

_____ **4.** Earthquakes can always be predicted.

_____ **5.** A storm warning means that the weather conditions are right for a storm
to form.

_____ **6.** A family disaster plan and disaster kit could save family members' lives.

_____ **7.** Sanitarians are people who collect trash from our neighborhoods
and businesses.

_____ **8.** Water treatment plants help ensure safe drinking water for people living
in or near large cities.

_____ **9.** Resources are materials from the environment that people use.

_____**10.** Conserving electricity is the only way to conserve natural resources.

List four ways in which local governments prepare
communities for approaching natural disasters.

11. _____

_____

_____

12. _____

_____

_____

13. _____

_____

_____

14. _____

_____

_____

Harcourt Brace School Publishers

Every family needs a disaster kit. Consider the items that would be most useful to your family during a blizzard. List four of those items on the lines below, and give reasons they are important.

15. _____

_____

16. _____

_____

17. _____

_____

18. _____

_____

Protecting our environment is the responsibility of every citizen. Decide how each resource or product found in the chart below could be reduced, reused, or recycled.

Resource/ Product	Reduce	Reuse	Recycle
19. water			
20. paper			
21. plastic			

Harcourt Brace School Publishers

The human body is harmed by air, water, and noise pollution. Complete the diagram below by naming five ways human health can be affected by pollution.

22. skin

_____

_____

_____

_____

23. ears

_____

_____

_____

_____

24. lungs

_____

_____

_____

_____

25. heart

_____

_____

_____

26. intestines

_____

_____

_____

_____

Harcourt Brace School Publishers

Name _____ Date _____

Chapter Project Evaluation Sheet (Teacher)

Chapter
9

Rubric for Evaluating Student Performance
on the Chapter 9 Project

Project: Make a disaster plan brochure
Purpose: To gather and organize information to show how to react in the event of a
natural disaster during school hours; to develop work skills; to use what is
learned from the project in everyday life

Use the indicators below to help you determine the student's overall score.

Level 3
The student fulfills the purpose of the project in an exemplary way.

_____ Gathers information from a variety of sources

_____ Organizes information to demonstrate a thorough understanding of how to react in
the event of a natural disaster during school hours

_____ Works alone with initiative or works cooperatively with others

_____ Communicates ideas clearly and effectively through a disaster plan brochure

_____ Demonstrates strong ability to apply the information in the disaster plan brochure
to everyday life

Level 2
The student fulfills the purpose of the project in a satisfactory way.

_____ Gathers information from more than one source

_____ Organizes information to demonstrate a reasonable understanding of how to react
in the event of a natural disaster during school hours

_____ Works alone with initiative or works cooperatively with others much of the time

_____ Communicates ideas reasonably, clearly, and effectively through a disaster plan
brochure

_____ Demonstrates some ability to apply the information in the disaster plan brochure to
everyday life

Level 1
The student does not fulfill the purpose of the project.

_____ Gathers insufficient information or uses only one source

_____ Fails to organize information to demonstrate adequate understanding of how to
react in the event of a natural disaster during school hours

_____ Lacks initiative when working alone or fails to work cooperatively

_____ Has difficulty communicating clear, complete ideas through a disaster plan brochure

_____ Demonstrates little ability to apply the information in the disaster plan brochure to
everyday life

Student's overall score _____
Teacher comments:

Harcourt Brace School Publishers

Chapter 9 • Community Health   **Assessment Guide • 53**

Chapter 1 Test

Setting Goals

page 18
1. b,c
2. a
3. d
4. b
5. d
6. Revise your plan if necessary.
7. Make a plan that includes short-term goals.

page 19
8. F
9. T
10. T
11. F
12. T
13. T
14. T
15. F
16. T
17. F
18. a
19. b
20. c

page 20
21. Know what stress feels like and what causes it.
22. When you expect a stressful situation, prepare to handle it.
23. Learn to release tension.
24. Focus on one step at a time.
25. Agree that you disagree.
26. Listen to all sides of the conflict.
27. Brainstorm solutions.
28. Choose a solution.
29. to ski this winter
30. to participate in physical therapy every day

Chapter 2 Test

Patterns of Growth

page 22
1. F
2. T
3. T
4. T
5. F
6. T
7. F
8. F
9. T

Answers to questions 10 and 11 will vary. Possible answers are shown.

10. His parents' divorce is not his fault; it's OK to have all kinds of feelings; he doesn't have to take sides; he can talk to a trusted adult or to a friend whose parents have also divorced.

11. She can be patient; she can remember that this is a new experience for everyone involved; she can let new family membrs have their way occasionally; she can be honest and respectful about her feelings; she can listen carefully to family members; she can follow family rules.

page 23
12. mitosis
13. chromosomes
14. heredity
15. dominant
16. nucleus
17. ovum
18. fetus
19. pituitary gland
20. thyroid gland
21. pancreas
22. ovaries
23. testes

page 24
24. Answers will vary. Sample answers: a growth spurt; shoulders will grow wider; body will become more muscular and strong; his voice will change; he will grow hair on different parts of his body; sweat glands will become more active; acne may develop.

25. During adolescence, the endocrine glands don't release hormones at a steady rate. Alberto's moods change as the levels of hormones in his body change.

26. Answers will vary. Sample answers: relationships; school requirements; thoughts about the future; desire for more privacy.

27. Answers will vary. Sample answers: to get regular exercise; to eat a healthful diet; to get enough rest; to abstain from alcohol, tobacco, and drugs.

Chapter 3 Test

Health and Fitness

page 26
1. SPF
2. epidermis
3. sweat glands
4. pores
5. hair follicles
6. dermis
7. c
8. b
9. a
10. e

page 27
11. Possible answers: advertiser is suggesting that product purchase increases popularity; bold lettering and clever language distract from the real message; provides no information about the quality or effectiveness of the product.
12. enamel
13. pulp
14. bone
15. crown
16. dentin
17. root

page 28
18. F
19. T
20. T
21. F
Answers to questions 22–25 will vary. Sample answers are shown.
22. Iris—opens and closes to adjust the amount of light that enters the eye.
23. Lens—focuses the light to form an image on the retina; retina—produces electrical signals that travel to the brain.
24. Wear safety goggles; never look directly into the sun; wear safety sunglasses.
25. Wear ear plugs or ear protectors; avoid mowing lawns for long periods of time.

Chapter 4 Test

Preparing Healthful Foods

page 30
1. g
2. f
3. j
4. a
5. d
6. b
7. i
8. c
9. h
10. e

page 31
11. Fats, oils, and sweets provide few nutrients and many Calories.
12. Milk, cheese, yogurt, and other dairy products supply protein, fats, carbohydrates, and minerals such as calcium and potassium.
13. Nuts, dried beans, eggs, fish, poultry, and meat are high in protein and may be rich in vitamins and minerals.
14. Vegetables are good sources of vitamins, minerals, fiber, and carbohydrates.
15. Fruits have little fat or cholesterol and are rich in fiber, minerals, vitamins, and carbohydrates.
16. Breads, cereals, rice, and pasta are made from grains. They contain complex carbohydrates, fiber, minerals, proteins, and vitamins. They are low in fat and cholesterol.

page 32
17. Anemia—a condition that makes it difficult for the blood to carry oxygen
18. weak bones
19. poor night vision; dry, inflamed eyes; loss of appetite; diarrhea; lowered resistance to disease
20. weakness, aches and pains, swollen gums, excessive bleeding
21. F
22. T
23. F
24. T
25. T
26. T
27. F
28. F

Chapter 5 Test

Controlling Disease

page 34
1. c
2. a
3. b
4. d
5. c
6. b
7. d
8. a

page 35

Causes of Infectious Diseases	Types of Infectious Diseases
10. viruses	9. influenza
11. protozoa	12. common cold
13. fungi	14. AIDS
	15. hepatitis

16. F
17. T
18. T
19. F
20. T
21. F
22. T
23. T
24. F
25. T

page 36
26. insulin
27. cardiovascular diseases
28. carcinogens
29. tumor
Answers to questions 30–34 will vary. Sample answers are shown.
30. avoiding pathogens by washing regularly;
31. exercising regularly;
32. eating a balanced diet;
33. getting enough sleep;
34. lowering stress; avoiding tobacco

Chapter 6 Test

Drugs and Health

page 38
1. addiction
2. side effects
3. over-the-counter medicines
4. dosage
5. drug dependence
6. drug
7. prescription medicines
8. medicines
9. tolerance
10. withdrawal

page 39
11. T
12. F
13. T
14. T
15. F
16. Heavy use can cause nervousness, sleeplessness, and dependency.
17. depression, shortness of breath, severe chest pain, seizures, death
18. Disrupt messages from the brain that control movement, thought, and speech; can shut down the brain completely.
19. Can make a person sleepy, habit-forming, cause lack of energy and lack of concentration, can shut down the brain completely.

page 40
Answers to questions 20–29 will vary. Sample answers are shown.
20. dependence, immediate effects on the body
21. problems with health and appearance
22. problems with motivation, withdrawal symptoms
23. social and emotional problems
24. tolerance, overdose
25. heart palpitations, breathing problems, dizziness, headaches
26. damage to the kidney, liver, blood, and nervous system; tolerance; death
27. LSD
28. PCP
29. They are illegal; getting more of the drug becomes a priority; drugs can be deadly; they can make a person very ill; they can keep a young person's body from maturing properly.

Chapter 7 Test

Tobacco and Alcohol

page 42

1. F
2. T
3. T
4. T
5. T
6. T
7. F
8. F
9. T
10. F
11. Possible answers: can cause watery eyes, burning noses, asthma attacks, heart disease, cancers, and death.
12.–13. Answers will vary. Sample answers are shown:
    raise a person's blood pressure and heart rate; cause diseases of the gums and teeth; cause sores in the mouth, throat, and stomach that can lead to cancers

page 43

14.–15. Answers will vary. Sample answers are shown:
    use nicotine gum or a nicotine skin patch; contact a counseling or support group
16. b
17. d
18. c
19. c
20. a
21. d
22. a
23. c

page 44

Answers to questions 24–30 will vary. Sample answers are shown.

24. Say no in a calm, clear voice and change the subject;
25. Say no, and give a reason such as the fact that alcohol is a dangerous substance for everyone.
26. Walk away; suggest something else to do.
27. Using these products won't make you energetic and won't make you have more fun; people using these products may smell bad and suffer from serious health problems.
28. These ads never show how hard it is to quit using these products; these ads never show how much money people waste as a result of drinking or smoking; these ads never mention that people get injured or killed from using these products.
29. They are trained to work with alcoholics and their families; they work one-on-one to help people quit drinking.
30. This group helps families and friends of alcoholics deal with the problems created by alcoholism.

Chapter 8 Test

Safety and First Aid

page 46
1. c
2. d
3. a
4. d
5. a
6. b
7. a
8. d
9. c
10. c

page 47
11. water
12. extra clothing
13. blankets
14. canned food
15. battery-powered radio and extra batteries
16. scissors and tweezers
17. bandages
18. hand cleaner and wipes
19. plastic bags
20. antiseptic ointment

Answers to questions 21–28 will vary. Sample answers are shown.
21. f; bring toys, bicycles, tools indoors; cover windows with boards and tape; close drapes; move inland if advised.

page 48
22. a; stay indoors; take cover under a heavy table; stand in a strong doorframe; stay away from furniture that may topple over.
23. e; stay away from all windows; get below ground, under stairs, under a heavy table, or in a basement corner; get in a bathroom or in a closet.
24. Sprain: Rest the ankle; apply ice; compress the injured ankle; elevate the ankle.
    Hypothermia: Call 911; stop the heat loss.
25. Burns: Stop the burning; cool the burn; cover the burn.
    Choking: If the person can, let him or her cough up the object. Otherwise, give one or more abdominal thrusts.
26. Keep it light and go slow; find a way to walk away.
27. Back off; avoid being alone.
28. Talk about it with an adult.

Chapter 9 Test

Community Health

page 50

1. F
2. T
3. F
4. F
5. F
6. T
7. F
8. T
9. T
10. F

Answers to questions 11–18 will vary. Sample answers are shown.

11. Teach people about disasters.
12. Find emergency shelters. Buy and maintain material and equipment.
13. Plan ways to warn the community.
14. Plan routes for people to follow.

page 51

15. candles for light, matches to light candles, flashlights for light
16. batteries for flashlight, cellular phone to talk to people
17. bottled water to drink, canned food to eat, can opener to open cans of food
18. blankets for warmth, warm clothes to wear

Resource/Product	Reduce	Reuse	Recycle
19. water	turn off water while brushing teeth		
20. paper	don't use paper plates or towels	reuse gift wrap when possible; use old envelopes and partially used sheets of paper as scrap paper	recycle newspaper and other recyclable paper
21. plastic	buy fewer products in plastic containers	reuse clean plastic bottles to store extra water	recycle all recyclable plastics

page 52

22. Chemicals from coal and oil furnaces can cause skin cancer.
23. Noise pollution can damage human hearing.
24. Chemicals in the air can damage lungs.
25. Fumes from motor vehicles can cause heart disease.
26. Water pollution can cause many intestinal problems in humans.